GRANTHAM
THROUGH TIME
John Pinchbeck

AMBERLEY PUBLISHING

Acknowledgements

Thanks to everyone who lent me their precious photographs including: Sheila Clarke, Barrie Cox, Ruth Crook, Ron Crowson, Dave Fardell, Vaughan Hardy, Keith Harrison, Fred Leadbetter, Dave Maltby, Mike Matsell, Peter Nicholls, Sue Redmile, Cath Rowson, Stuart Watts and the *Grantham Journal*.

Grantham House

First published 2012

Amberley Publishing
The Hill, Stroud
Gloucestershire, GL5 4EP

www.amberley-books.com

Copyright © John Pinchbeck, 2012

The right of John Pinchbeck to be identified as the Author of this work has been asserted in accordance with the Copyrights, Designs and Patents Act 1988.

ISBN 978 1 4456 0807 5

British Library Cataloguing in Publication Data.
A catalogue record for this book is available from the British Library.

Typeset in 9.5pt on 12pt Celeste.
Typesetting by Amberley Publishing.
Printed in the UK.

Introduction

While Westgate, Market Place and the Castlegate areas hardly change, the main street, from North Parade to South Parade is in a state of constant change.

Grantham's constant is St Wulfram's Church, built by the Greyfriars and one of the highest spires in the country. The Knights Templar who were brilliant financiers – the hedge fund managers of their day – built the Angel Hotel in the twelfth century, while the sixteenth-century Grantham House and the seventeenth-century White House in Brownlow Street remain – although much changed over the years.

Road improvements during the eighteenth century placed Grantham firmly on the new coaching routes which were being developed. Numerous inns opened which provided fresh horses for travellers, and then in the 1790s the Grantham Canal opened taking grain to Nottingham and returning with barges full of coal and fertiliser.

The next big boost in Grantham's economy was thanks to Sir William Manners, who in 1804 invested money in five turnpike roads leading to Grantham. Wool remained the mainstay of the town's economy for 800 years until the early nineteenth century when a young farrier set up in business on London Road. Richard Hornsby began on the Great North Road, in Spittlegate, before it became part of Grantham. Hornsby also accepted repair work for farmers, and noticed how inefficient their equipment was. Knowing he could do better he began to make them.

By the 1840s Hornsby's was producing steam engines, steel ploughs, binders and reapers. Under the leadership of manager David Roberts, it went on to develop the compression engine which was in full production by 1892 three years before Rudolf Diesel 'invented' it. He built the first diesel tractor and successfully developed the track vehicle although no one could see a use for this until the Great War for the tank.

James Coultas meanwhile, had settled on a parallel strategy, starting in Union Street and moving to Station Road (pre-station). Coultas stuck to what he knew best, concentrating on quality agricultural equipment and castings and did not expand to the same extent.

The arrival of the railway in the 1850s played a crucial role and became a major employer at its loco depot, Springfield Road.

Mid-Victorian Grantham was running out of space so in 1879 the Borough Extension Act was introduced. This added Spittlegate to the south, much of Harrowby east of the river, part of Somerby (New Somerby) Little Gonerby (around New Street & Brook Street), the Grange, Earle's Fields, plus Houghton and Walton to the west. High Street, Watergate, Market Place, Westgate and the north-east end of London Road, then saw a boom in shop building. A new breed of shop began to appear on Grantham's High Street, department stores – all run by local enterprising businessmen. We also get our first 'national' company moving in – regional at that time really – Boots. It set a trend by pulling down an old Tudor building for its purpose-built premises.

The First World War had a massive effect on Grantham. It became a garrison town with two Army camps, Belton and Harrowby. All the land east of the Witham from what is now Wyndham Park to Belton Park, as far back as Alma Park was under canvas or wooden huts as either Belton or Harrowby Army camps.

In the late 1920s and early 1930s the town sank into the doldrums, hit by the worldwide depression. Ruston & Hornsby's was struggling and only a last ditch stand stopped the company closing the Grantham factory. Other councillors rolled up their sleeves and brought in new industries including arms-maker BMARCo, crane makers R. H. Neal, Bjorlows tannery and brokered the creation of Aveling-Barford.

Although it suffered badly from bombing in the Second World War, most of it fell on industrial and housing areas, leaving commerce unscathed. But where the Luftwaffe failed, the bulldozers moved in the 1950s/60s. Old Georgian and Victorian buildings made way for modern, and many think soulless ones. Watergate took the biggest hammering. The northern gateway of High Street had been a problem once cars, and especially lorries were introduced, so in 1960 it was decided to widen it.

The 1970s/80s saw much of the town's engineering base disappear. Ruston & Hornsby, Grantham Boiler & Crank, Bjorlows, Coles Cranes, BMARCo and British Leyland-owned Barford's either closed or were in terminal decline.

The prestigious George Hotel closed and although the shell remained it became a shopping centre with a fitness studio, educational and recruitment offices.

The ever-changing economic climate has made Grantham an ever-changing town.

St Wulfram's Church from the Walled Garden of Grantham House

Woolworths

Dewhurst butcher's, the *Grantham Journal* and O'Brien's cycle shop all came down in 1957 to make way for the new Woolworths store which incorporated a new *Journal* reception area. Woolworths closed in 2011 replaced by B&M.

High Street I

Comedian Benny Hill visited Grantham in 1957 and High Street was lined with fans. He was there to promote Alice M. Griffin's hair salon. The top picture shows the east side with crowds not only on the pavements but peering from windows. Little has changed apart from the intrusion of a modern building among the Victorian ones.

Civic Parade

The civic parade on Mayor's Sunday in May 1957. The Red Cross contingent is marching along St Peter's Hill, showing how much it has changed in half a century. Cinemas Granada and The Picture House are now both long gone, the International Stores, the Railway Tavern and photographer John MacKay are just a memory. The Rainbow Café, a milk bar where girls in flared skirts met boys in drainpipe trousers, has also been consigned to history.

High Street II

The Midland Bank, High Street, was pulled down in 1933 together with Foster's tobacconist. In their place, national clothing store Marks & Spencer built a new shop, opened in August, where nothing cost more than 25p. The bank transferred its business to Westgate. The man is standing outside Geo Mills tailoring shop. Marks & Spencer closed its Grantham branch in 2011 and at the time of writing is still an empty shell, while after a spell as Burton's, Mills became Lloyds Pharmacy in 2011.

Whipple's Motor Dealership

Whipple's motor dealership was opposite the George Hotel in 1908 when the top picture was taken. It was formed as a cycle maker and repairer but the core business was a haberdashery in Watergate. When that store was destroyed by fire in 1918 the company concentrated on motor cars and built the biggest garage in the midlands on the gutted site.

Waterloo House

For about 170 years, Waterloo House was a major feature on Grantham High Street, with its distinctive first floor windows. In 1911, it was owned by Garratt's, who opened the store in a former grocer's shop on the corner of Guildhall Street. Departments included haberdashery, drapery, gown and costume, clothing, knitting and embroidery silk. After the Second World War, it became divided into separate shops until it was demolished in 1985 and a modern building was erected on the site.

Dickinson's General Stores

Sandwiched between the Angel and Royal Hotel and the Cross Swords pub when the top picture was taken in 1910 was Dickinson's General Stores, known as the Noah's Ark because of the model ark above the doorway. During the 1950s, when demolition in the Vine Street and Watergate area was rife, the Cross Swords was bulldozed and Wilkinson's hardware built on the site, while Dickinson's became part of the Angel & Royal Hotel and is now Simply Bertie's Bistro.

Newcombe's Chemists

The quaint premises of Newcombe's was demolished in 1932 to make way for Burton's, opposite the Angel & Royal Hotel. The tailoring chain's art deco building opened a year later and remained until moving to the former Geo Mills shop, opposite the George Hotel, in the 1980s. The distinctive building remains but is now occupied by Addaction Lincolnshire, a treatment service for the effects of addiction.

The George Hotel

The George Hotel interior in the 1920s when it was Grantham's premier hotel. The original hostelry was destroyed in a major blaze from Butchers Row to Guildhall Street in the 1770s after which the huge Georgian edifice we know today was built on the site. During the great era of stagecoach traffic, the inn flourished.

In 1923 a ballroom was added and the archway was fitted with a revolving door. It became a quality hotel with forty-six bedrooms, a restaurant and a ballroom for many local functions including wedding receptions, Christmas parties and annual balls. It closed in 1989.

A shopping mall was built on the car park, the ground floor converted to shops and offices and a new façade were constructed on Guildhall Street. It was renamed St Peter's Place, but this error was soon rectified and it became known as the George Centre.

The *Grantham Journal*

The *Grantham Journal* as seen from what later became Greenwoods Row car park but at that time it was an orchard. It was originally a coaching inn called the Mail Hotel, although the local newspaper has been on the site since the 1860s. The old buildings were pulled down in 1957 to make way for Woolworths and the *Journal* buildings we see today.

Bus Station

The bus station which ran between Welham Street and St Peter's Hill opened in 1933. It had a kiosk for fruit and other refreshments as well as covered waiting rooms and shelters. The station served the town well until the district council saw the chance of using the land to build more offices and a debating chamber for itself, so in 1984 a new terminus was incorporated into the new Isaac Newton Centre, on Wharf Road. *Above*: A school bus is allowed to leave the strike torn bus station on St Peter's Hill, in 1953, but shoppers were left stranded. Behind Platform 10 is the old police station, before it moved to Stonebridge, St Catherine's Road. *Below*: The council chamber and committee rooms which replaced it.

London Road

A football match at the old London Road ground, with its infamous slope in 1961. At the time, there was no concrete terracing at the top end, just cinders. Along the left was the 'Shed', low roofed and standing only, as was the 'Witham End' on the far side. One of the ground's best known features was the row of poplar trees. To the right of the football pitch was the cricket square, as Grantham Cricket Club used the whole ground in summer.

The ground was redeveloped for Safeway supermarket in the late 1980s and a new era dawned for Grantham Town Football Club at the Meres stadium in the early 1990s, while the cricketers moved to Gorse Lane. Safeway was taken over by Wm Morrison who in turn sold it to Sainsbury's, which now occupies the site.

Grantham Motor Company

Grantham Motor Company's art deco style building in 1990, the year before the company moved out to Spittlegate Level. It was built for the company in 1923 and little changed in nearly seventy years, save for corporate imagery. The clock, which had been a timepiece for workers going to Ruston and Hornsby as well as Aveling Barford, for many years, was electric – powered by a wind-up clockwork generator. Unfortunately it wasn't saved when the building was demolished in 1999. The site became a retail park, selling carpets, frozen food and video rentals.

Grantham Town Football Club

More than 6,000 spectators turned out for Grantham Town FC's second preliminary FA Cup round in 1954 against Boston United. The Stumpites (Pilgrims) were two goals up before the break but a gallant fight back saw two goals in as many minutes to force a replay at the Shodfriars Lane ground which Town lost by a late goal.

The Blue Horse closed and was converted into a fish and chip shop while the car park and Grantham Bowls Club behind it became first Fat Lou's American diner and then Thai restaurant Siam Garden. You may just make out The Reaper on the corner of Oxford Street, which closed two years after the above picture was taken. For many years it was plumbers Pacey's.

North Road Garage

A Triumph Herald was hoisted 30 feet on top of North Road Garage's showroom, London Road, in 1967. The work was carried out by Coles Cranes whose factory was on Dysart Road. One of the town's senior dealerships, it began at Great Ponton in 1920. It moved to the former Mowbray's brewery site, London Road, Grantham, in 1963 and was opened by world motor racing champion Graham Hill, who drove for BRM. The houses next door were later knocked down to provide a forecourt for both NRG and neighbours Grantham Motor Company. NRG closed in 1982 and after various uses, the property together with the Barley Mow pub next door was pulled down and a retail park built in its place.

Ruston & Hornsby I

Ruston & Hornsby's London Road factory in 1971, which stood idle following the closure; Alfred Wiseman had taken over the premises in 1962. It was planned to become a supermarket although that never materialised. The buildings found various uses, including a trades fair, but in the 1980s they were bought by a consortium of local businessmen, demolished, and a retail park created with MFI and B&Q. On the corner of Spring Gardens, once the bustling foundry, was motor dealers Hindmarch, later Guildhall Motors and eventually Will Bond plumbing.

Nag's Head

The original Nag's Head stood on the corner of Wharf Road and London Road before being pulled down in 1883 and the building we know today put in its place. In the 1990s, the owners had ambitious plans for extending the pub but when these were turned down by the district council, it was sold and became a restaurant downstairs with apartments on the upper floors. After a spell as One on Wharf, it became ethnic restaurant Gurkha Square.

Bombing I

Seven people were killed and sixteen injured when four high-explosive bombs hit Ruston & Hornsby's east side works, London Road, in 1940. The erection shop and drawing office were destroyed. Nearby Parker's shop, the Joiners Arms and Steel & Hubbard's garage were razed to the ground and fourteen other buildings were damaged. Hornsby's erection shop was hit by the first bomb and the drawing office by the second. The third fell into the road outside Parker's shop and the Joiners. The final bomb hit the garage in the Manners' Arms yard. It brought tiles from the pub and the Spotted Cow opposite crashing down.

The workshops were partially rebuilt but the blacksmith's shop was destroyed in a fire some twenty years later. The site was taken over by John Lee (Sacks) but in the 1980s it was cleared for a filling station. Contractors working on it had to stop work when they unearthed fifty skeletons from the thirteenth-century St Leonard's leper colony.

Royal Wedding

A party celebrating the Royal Wedding between Prince Charles and Princess Diana was held on the Manners Arms car park, London Road (corner of Springfield Road) in 1981. The pub, named after the family resident at Belvoir Castle, was Victorian and built in the mid-nineteenth century to accommodate the boom at Ruston & Hornsby. It closed at the turn of the twenty-first century and was pulled down in about 2004 to make way for Pizza Hut, which still occupies the site.

Ruston & Hornsby II

Ruston & Hornsby's foundry in 1928, at the curiously named Spring Gardens. It was dark, in places too hot, others too cold and workmen aged prematurely. There were also lots of accidents with molten metal. It was dismal with black sand on the floor and in the pores of everyone's skin. The foundry closed in 1956 with the loss of ninety jobs and the work was transferred to Lincoln. The building was used for storage until 1973 when it was pulled down and a car showroom was erected on the site.

John Lee's Warehouse

Huge flames were seen for miles around as they engulfed John Lee's warehouse, London Road, in 1960, causing £50,000 damage. Hundreds of tons of stock were destroyed and only a charred shell of the former Hornsby's blacksmiths shop remained.

The alarm was raised at 9 p.m. on a Saturday and eight fire crews were soon on the scene. The heat was so intense it caused the main wall to bulge and sway, putting firemen in constant danger. The asbestos roofing exploded, sending long tongue-like flames high into the clear night sky. The main road was blocked for hours by fire engines and there were thousands of spectators, as the pubs and dance halls turned out. Firefighters risked their lives on the upper storey, yet the only injury was a twisted ankle. Even more incredible was that the blaze stopped less than a metre from a tank containing 10,000 litres of petrol. A tank of paraffin also survived.

Union Court

Some of the old houses in Union Court, Inner Street, were demolished in 1934. They lacked what we now regard as basic amenities such as indoor toilets, fresh water and had ladders rather than stairs to reach the bedrooms. They were also notoriously damp, having been built in the 1830s as people left the land for the better wages being paid at local factories.

In 1964, as STD (Subscriber Trunk Calling) was introduced, Post Office Telephones (later BT) moved from St Peter's Hill to a purpose-built automatic telephone exchange, in Inner Street. It closed in 1992 and the work transferred to Peterborough. It is now a BT engineering depot.

Little Has Changed

At first it would seem only the usage of these buildings has changed since the first photograph was taken in 1892, apart from the timbers of the Malt Shovels being exposed. Closer inspection shows that the archway of this former coaching inn, now a Chinese restaurant, has been moved. This happened during rebuilding in the 1960s.

Westgate Cottages

There was an outcry in 1981 when the council declared it was to bulldoze Westgate Cottages as being unfit to live in. Many people believed they could have been renovated and turned into ideal homes for couples with no family. However, demolished they were and in their place grew Great Northern Court.

Westgate

The angle's the same and the content almost identical in these two pictures taken sixty years apart. Both, one from the 1950s, the other in 2012, shows the Mid-Lent Fair at the end of Westgate, stopped to allow the flow of traffic from Dysart Road and Stanton Street (now leading from Morrison's car park).

Market Place I

The Cross in the Market Place marked the place where market tolls were payable. It was pulled down by John Manners, Lord of the Manor, in 1779, but an action was brought against him for the trespass, and he was compelled to restore it the following year as Royal Proclamations were to be made from it. But that didn't stop his son William repeating this in 1796, who also was forced to put it back. The Manners family tried yet again in 1884 when this time they replaced it with a granite obelisk as seen above in the 1904 picture. However, in 1910 the Cross was returned and re-erected by builder G. E. Priest following a campaign by the deputy mayor, William Plumb.

Most of the buildings remain, although Broughton's was pulled down in the 1900s and replaced by the building – reflecting the style of one built by Boots next door to the Angel – now housing Italian restaurant Sorrento.

Market Place II

A busy Grantham Market in about 1905 when most of the stock was transported by horse and cart or hand barrow. The market is still held every Saturday and the Market Place is one area that has seen little change other than cosmetic.

Market Place III

The Market Place in 1911, before the Blue Sheep and the market hall were demolished to open up Conduit Lane and Union Street. The Blue Lion was a public house until 1969 when it became offices. On the far left, Ogdens, which had been a garden shop for nearly a century, closed in the 1980s. It became first an antique shop then a recruitment agency.

Market Place IV

Before the days of supermarkets, most groceries were bought from either the corner shop or the larger stores such as Lipton's and International Stores. The stores always had a wooden (later glass) counter with shelves in the background. Often there would be a bacon slicer where rashers were sliced off the haunch and sugar was weighed in front of you and poured into a plain blue bag. Only the staff handled the goods until they were paid for.

This is Melias, the premises the Market Place American Pizza fish and chip shop now occupies. The picture was taken in February 1953. From left: Christa Tooke, Mary Sharp, Sheila Clarke, and manager John Seymour. Today the signage is far more flashy.

Wharf Road

The public slipper baths on Wharf Road are shown in this photograph from the early 1900s. It became unfashionable once modern houses were built with their own bathrooms. It was knocked down in the mid-1980s as part of the Isaac Newton Centre development. The Baptist Church behind it is still there – although it is a different one! The church was built in the 1880s but after suffering subsidence had to be rebuilt in 1930.

The Golden Fleece

The Golden Fleece annual outing in the 1950s was a special day out for many families who couldn't afford proper holidays. In this case they were taken by Pulfreys of Great Gonerby. The pub, on the corner of Wharf Road and Grantley Street, went through a couple of name changes in later life. It became Warthogs, named after landlord Tony 'Warthog' Willows and Churchills. After seeing in the twenty-first century it closed as a pub and was converted to flats.

ESTABLISHED 1842—
—95 Years

HOUSE COALS, STEAM COALS, NUTS, SLACKS,
ANTHRACITE, GAS COKE, FURNACE COKE,
FIREWOOD, HARDWOOD LOGS,
KINDLING WOOD.

"WITCH" FIRELIGHTERS.
COALITE—THE SMOKELESS FUEL.

TRUCK LOADS TO ANY STATION.
DELIVERIES EVERYWHERE.

Wm. Clarke & Son, Ltd.

Coal and Coke Factors and Merchants,
8, Wharf Road,   TEL. 119.
                   GRANTHAM.

Also at Lincoln, Leicester, E. Markham, Cotham, John O'
Gaunt, Scalford, Digby, Great Dalby, Crow Park, Tuxford,
London (all districts), Ruskington, Harby, Clifton, Branston,
and Heighington, Blankney and Metheringham, Swinderby,
Newark, Heckington, Helpringham, etc.

William Clarke
An advertisement from the 1930s for William Clarke, coal merchants on Wharf Road, Brewery Hill Corner. The building is still there, and was home to several other coal merchants before the fuel became unfashionable. It is now an East European food store.

Wallwork's

Wallwork's furniture shop in Wharf Road awaiting demolition in 1982. The shop had previously been C. W. Dixon, also selling furniture. This, together with neighbours Plamore Sports and an unusual pair of houses, was sacrificed for a new bus station.

Welby Street

The east side of Welby Street was already disappearing when this photograph was taken in 1982. The car is coming out of Greenwoods Row, then connected to the car park and Guildhall Street. John Lee's offices had already come down. In the background, Welby Street School awaits demolition. It had ceased as an educational establishment just before the war although used only temporarily during it. In later years it had been put to industrial use and storage by local businesses including Grantham Electrical Engineering. By 1985, it was all undercover, as part of the Isaac Newton Centre.

Welby Street

Welby Street in 1983 looking towards Westgate. The tall building is the Plough Inn. Only the building at the end, with the rendered side towards camera, has survived. Originally it was wine merchants Johnson & Basker, but is now a slot machine palace.

Watergate

Watergate had been a prime shopping street up to the mid-twentieth century as the 1920s picture shows. Unfortunately, in post-war years the car took over and the eastern side was bulldozed to widen what was then the Great North Road. Watergate House was built and a small park opened although the latter was short-lived, becoming a car park. Then in the late 1960s, the bottom half of the west side, north of Whipple's Garage (later Kwik-Fit), was knocked down to create Key Markets superstore.

Collards

Ironmongers Collards had been around for half a century when it closed in 1986. It was a place where you could buy one screw, with a choice of Whitworth, BSF, BA, etc. It also sold guns and cartridges. The site on which Whipple's stands in the earlier photograph was once a notorious pub called the Swan & Salmon, which closed in the 1880s. Ironically, by the 1990s it was part of a pub again, this time the Gatehouse which eventually became the Playhouse.

Whipple's

Whipple's haberdashery in 1897 celebrating Queen Victoria's Diamond Jubilee. The business was destroyed by fire in 1918 and rebuilt as a motor dealership set further back from the road. This was a foresight on the part of the council, although the subsequent authority some 30 years later decided instead to knock down the other side of the road in its bid to widen the street. The new garage was the biggest motor workshop in the Midlands at the time. When Whipple's closed in the 1980s, it was taken over by Kwik-Fit.

Harrison's

This block including Harrison's osier, pram and luggage shop were demolished in 1967, to make way for Key Markets supermarket. Key Market became Gateway which closed in 2000. The premises was taken over by German chain Lidl.

Grantham Charity Rag

Grantham Charity Rag on Saturday 14 September 1929, passing through North Street. These were large terraced houses not unlike the ones around the corner in Brook Street. They were demolished in 1979 and replaced by Premier Court.

Guildhall Street

Guildhall Street in 1976 before Guildhall Car Company (previously Campion Depot) was demolished. The company moved to London Road. The wall on the left was demolished, and the former Guinness bottling plant was converted into shops and a café.

Blue Court

Blue Court, which had one outdoor toilet for every two houses and was last occupied in the 1960s, was ruled unfit for habitation. In 1977 it was agreed to demolish them. However, five years later they were reprieved and converted to boutiques and cafés. This remains one of the few areas of town which has seldom seen an empty shop.

Swinegate I

Swinegate was the original main street through Grantham and is largely unspoilt, having seen hardly any development for well over a century, save for the King's School extension which technically is on Broad Street. It is dominated by St Wulfram's Church and is a mixture of mainly Georgian housing with Victorian intrusions. There is little between these two pictures, other than traffic. Swinegate not only suffers from road vehicles, but the introduction of signage and signals.

Wall

The wall with the medieval archway leading to the houses in Artichokes Yard, was knocked down in the 1960s to make way for the hideous car showroom which sits there today. The Artichokes pub to its right closed in 1921 but got a new lease of life in the 1970s, which saw the rendering removed and the timber beams exposed. It is now offices.

The Blue Pig

On the corner of Vine Street and Swinegate, the Blue Pig is one of the town's oldest buildings, but not the oldest pub. In fact, there is no evidence that it was licensed premises until 1826 and was probably converted from a range of cottages. Yet it hid its secret for centuries. It wasn't until 1925, while examining the building for internal improvements, when architect Wilfred Bond discovered it was originally a stone building with an oak-framed upper storey. The stone walls were uncovered and pointed while the timbers in the upper storey were exposed and the spaces plastered. Only four years earlier it had been recommended for closure by Licensing Magistrates who said: 'The Blue Pig is the most undesirable type of house. It has badly arranged rooms, is low, dark and badly ventilated and altogether a building in bad condition.'

The Crown and Anchor

The Crown and Anchor, originally just the Crown, was built in 1794. It was one of the town's oldest pubs when it closed in 1936. It was then used for storage, latterly by motor dealers R. M. Wright. It was demolished in the 1990s and replaced by King's Court Nursing Home.

Swinegate II

A link with the town's theatrical history ended when the old billiards saloon, in Swinegate, was pulled down in 1952 to make way for a filling station. The building on the corner of Brook Street was owned by Lou Musson, who wanted to extend his new Empire Garage. It had a varied history. Built in 1800, it had also been a theatre, gymnasium, sale room, meeting room and most recently a warehouse for a vegetable wholesaler. Eventually Empire was taken over by Save as a filling station. When that closed at the turn of the millennium, it was bought by King's School and new classrooms were built.

King's School

The original King's School was where a young Isaac Newton was a pupil. He is even alleged to have carved his initials in a window sill on the premises. Since the school developed in the early twentieth century, newer buildings have been introduced and at first the old school was a chapel. It has also been the assembly hall, a school theatre, a gymnasium and is now the library.

Brownlow Street

Children in today's picture of Brownlow Street can't afford to stand around as their predecessors did at the turn of the twentieth century. Even on a controlled crossing, they have to be quick. Only one building remains from the picture taken in 1904 and that is the White House, now better known as Miss Fairish's Almshouse, which dates from before the English Civil War.

Wide Load

An iron dredging barge hauled by a Fowler B6 road locomotive brought traffic to a standstill in October 1933. The boat was on its way to London and although railway operator LNER was in charge of the move, it was far too big for rail. The cargo was too big to take through Chapel Street and had to go via Brownlow Street and Broad Street (below) before turning on to the Great North Road in North Street to continue its journey through town. On the right corner is the Sun Inn. Much of this area was demolished in the 1980s making way for Premier Court.

Vere Street

Vere Street from the north end in 1934 was crossed by James Street at about where the children are playing. At the end is the bottom of Watergate. They had long fallen into disrepair, bulldozed in the 1970s and eventually replaced by Premier Court.

Vere Court

The entrance to Vere Court from Broad Street in 1934. This was a notorious area and soon after this picture was taken, all but the house on the right, recently renovated, were demolished.

Roberts

Roberts shop and post office, North Parade, is best known as the birthplace of Prime Minister Margaret Thatcher. The above picture shows the iconic, deserted corner shop as a target for anti-unemployment protestors in 1981. Part of it had been used as an antique shop by dealer John Couzens. It became the Premier restaurant in the 1990s, and is now Living Health.

Margaret Thatcher

NUPE (National Union of Public Employees) members and four-year-old Rachael Pitt laid a wreath at Prime Minister Margaret Thatcher's birthplace in 1988. They were demanding more government money for the NHS. Although the NHS survived, the buildings behind them didn't. The large building is the Blue Bell Inn, on the corner of North Street and Barrowby Road. The building to the left is Leyland Cars dealer R. M. Wright. The site of the buildings is now part of a wider road and Asda car park.

Statue of Our Lady
The Statue of Our Lady in St Mary's Church, North Parade, was crowned as part of the 1951 May Day celebration by the May Queen Ann Murphy. Also there were parish priest Canon L. A. Arendzen and Father P. Downey (kneeling). The marble reredos and altar were torn down and used as hardcore in the building's extensions. It was replaced by a modern baptistery.

North Parade

Roy Levicks's garage, North Parade, seen here in 1960, was a landmark for many years with its roadside pumps, a relic from the early days of motoring. Following Mr Levick's retirement, it was demolished and replaced by flats, which although simple, at first glance fit in with the Georgian and early Victorian architecture. Just don't take a second glance.

Charles Street, 1934
Nothing remains of the street, Malt Hill, nor Manners Street which were all around this site. A new Manners Street was built, in a slightly different place.

Castlegate I

The Queen's Nurses, dedicated to looking after the sick poor in their own homes, opened a new home in Castlegate. The Queen Victoria Institute for Nurses had already become established in the town in 1901, when Mayor of Grantham, Tryner Lynn, launched the fund for the building to be a memorial to the monarch. Local companies furnished the Tudor-style building, which included four bedrooms, a bathroom and a toilet, with further sleeping space in the attic. It has since been incorporated into the offices of insurance brokers Russell Plaice & Partners.

Castlegate II

This 1960 photograph of Castlegate still shows the Beehive Inn on the left, but across the road is quite different. John Wallwork had begun to rebuild the area. Castlegate fisheries is almost opposite Pestell's, who were in the same business. Next to them was Isobel Melrose, who ran a sweetshop next to the Blue Cow which had recently been demolished. Mr Wallwork's furniture store eventually became Fine Fare supermarket. However, with the exception of the corner building Images, later the Castlegate pub, it all came down in recent years to become flats.

Middlemore Yard

Middlemore Yard in the 1930s looks normal enough but these were among the worst housing conditions in Grantham. It was built on the grounds of Middlemore House, which ran down to the River Witham. The house, which still stands almost unnoticed, was built by lawyer Richard Middlemore in the early 1700s. But the house and grounds were sold off some 150 years later when the family moved to Somerby Hall. Much of the grounds became covered with cheap, terraced homes. These houses were cleared in the late 1940s and now form part of the Conservative Club car park.

The Empire

Built in 1875, the Empire, George Street, closed in December 1954. Originally called the Theatre Royal & Opera House, it was also the home of the town's Salvation Army before the Citadel was built. It was destroyed by fire in 1888 but reopened three years later with seating for 1,250 customers as the Theatre Royal and Empire. By the time it closed, it was showing only old films, the maximum charge being two shillings (10p) for a seat in the circle. Having the largest floor area in town, there were ambitious plans to convert it into a ballroom but instead became a tyre-fitting centre for ATS (Associated Tyre Distributors) with its offices in George Street and a depot in East Street. The George Street side has been converted into flats.

East Street I

Empty cottages at the top of East Street, originally called Well Lane, in June 1937, which were pulled down and replaced by modern houses. The rest of the houses on the left were demolished in the 1960s to make way for a multi-level car park for Wallwork's furniture store. On the right, the tall building is the rear (stage end) of the Empire Theatre which became a tyre depot. In the distance is Pidcock's Maltings, Welham Street. The man with the handcart is a street cleaner, going to the depot at the end of the street, where the contents were tipped. In the contemporary picture, the theatre building remains (only lowered), modern housing is on the left and Pidcock's has been replaced by the Riverside housing scheme.

East Street II

Although several businesses had been powered by electricity since 1868, using their own generators, it was 1903 when Grantham's first power station in East Street was switched on. Its generators were able to supply businesses and private houses in High Street, Watergate, London Road, Wharf Road, Westgate, Castlegate and Swinegate.

It wasn't long before the council preferred all new lighting to be electric and gas street lighting was gradually replaced. By 1950 work began on a £14,000 scheme to replace all of Grantham's gas street lamps with electric ones, even the traditional dolphin gas lamp standards. The power station was closed when replaced by the National Grid, being demolished in the 1970s for a car park for Wallwork's furniture store. This in turn was pulled down and replaced by housing.

Grantham Railway Station I

Harlaxton Road railway bridge has scarcely changed a century after a major crash with any damage coming from lorries passing underneath rather than rail traffic. Fifteen passengers and crew were killed and sixteen injured when the 8.45 p.m. express from King's Cross to Edinburgh failed to make its scheduled stop at Grantham station in September 1906. It ploughed through the parapet of the bridge over Old Wharf Road. The Scotch Express, hauled by two-year-old Atlantic No. 276, surprised waiting passengers and post office workers as it thundered through the station. Within seconds there was an explosion and the air was filled with flames, smoke and debris. Crowds gathered along Harlaxton Road the following day to watch the heavy lifting cranes brought in to clear the lines.

Cattlemarket, Dysart Road, 1970

The area close to the railway embankment was sacrificed towards the end of the 1990s for Sankt Augustin Way. It was a downward spiral for the century old market after that. First it was hit by foot and mouth disease, followed by expensive demands from new regulations, so demolition men moved on to the 2.1-acre site, which had been a car park since the cattle market closed in December 2003. Owners, Buckminster Trust, allowed development as a retail park including flagship store Next.

Welham Street

The former car showroom and National Tyre Services (NTS) depot in Welham Street was boarded up awaiting demolition in 2004. Originally built in the late 1940s as a Mercedes Benz dealership, it was replaced by the Waterfront apartments development. The house and garden at the corner of Avenue Road were also casualties. The multi-storey car park opposite was yet to be built.

Corner of Avenue Road and Welham Street

No one was hurt in this collision between a Rover and a Riley Elf in 1959 although the latter was knocked over on to its side. It happened on the corner of Avenue Road and Welham Street, in front of Pidcock's maltings. But it did prove to be a big attraction, especially for the inquisitive young boys in the area. Pidcock's was demolished in the 1970s and replaced by Riverside housing complex.

Bridge End Road I
Bridge End Road post office in 1995 before it was demolished to make way for modern developments, which included the demolition of the adjacent service station. Almost as a memorial, a post box stands in front of the site.

Bridge End Road II
The end of the line for the Bridge End Road maltings in January 1969, making way for Gainsborough Corner filling station. It was previously owned by Joe Thompson and was bought by Lee and Grinling in 1930. It was a floor maltings for drying barley prior to malsting. The filling station closed in 2001 and the site became a McDonald's.

Bridge End Road III
Workmen dismantled the tower on the Bridge End Road Wesleyan Church, built in 1875 and closed at Christmas 1964. The assembly hall was redeveloped as a night club which ran for more than thirty years under various names. The club was demolished in 2004 and two buildings appeared in their place, Sally and Domino's Pizza.

Cold Harbour Lane

The houses on the left have changed little since a lorry collided with this lamppost in 1961. The rest is totally different. There is a filling station across the road where once were allotments and houses had been built at the bottom of Cold Harbour Lane. Trees have been cut down to build the houses have revealed the houses on Harrowby Road. And of course, the lampposts have been moved back from the road, to prevent it happening again.

St Mary's Catholic School

The former St Mary's Catholic School was used by the ARP (Air Raid Precautions) wardens during the Second World War. The school had moved to Sandon Road in 1928 as it needed far more space. It was built in 1859 on the site of one which had fallen down due to poor foundations. It has since been given a makeover, although you can still just see the faded brickwork where the wartime signage was cleaned off. In peacetime it has been a works' social club for both Reads and Kontaks, the Hugh More Club and is now church rooms.

Union Street I

Houses in Union Street are brightly decorated for the 1935 Civic Celebrations to mark 100 years of Grantham Borough Council. They were next door to the Joiners Arms. The houses have been replaced by Hunters Bar, formerly Maximum snooker club, while the pub was renamed the Nobody Inn.

Union Street II

These two large houses were in Union Street and are now hardcore for an Asda car park. They were pulled down in the 1960s to make way for the indoor swimming pool – later the leisure centre – and were roughly behind Leyland dealer R. M. Wright's workshop. This had previously been joiners Brown & Webb's workshop and Mr Brown once lived in the house with the bay window. He later sold the house to scrap merchant Charlie Spick.

George Pollard's Shop, Norton Street, 1984

The decrepit shop, a former bakery, supplied nearly every part the amateur car mechanic could wish for and at a very good price. It was pulled down in about 2004 and flats were built in its place. The building housing Grantham Organs was once the Norton Arms while the building opposite (left) was the Army Recruitment Office.

St John's Hall, Launder Terrace

These flats built in Launder Terrace at the turn of the twenty-first century replaced the former St John's church hall. This was originally Home House, built in 1870 by industrialist James Coultas. When the family sold up in 1934, the church, looking to build a church hall, snapped it up for £300. They had planned to build a large hall in the vicarage garden, fronting Station Road East. Instead they added an extension behind the house in Queen Street costing a further £900. Funds were raised by selling special bricks, each bearing the buyer's name. It was used as a dance studio until quite close to its demolition.

Station Road

A party of scouts march up Station Road (East) wearing their 'lemon squeezer' hats and shorts in 1955. Fashions, even for scouts, have changed. The building on the right was part of Ruston & Hornsby's engineering works which became Hilary Morgan Bridal Fashions. It was later demolished in 1998. The hoardings in the background disguise London Road cricket ground. The cricket club moved to Gorse Lane in the late 1980s and the old ground became a supermarket.

Grantham Railway Station II

There was still a water tower outside Grantham railway station in 1958, which became redundant with the withdrawal of steam locomotives. The Stationmaster's House is to the left of the picture. Both have since disappeared as more space was required for car parking.

Railway Yards

The railway yards, which once employed more than 1,000 men, were closing down and the coaling tower, which used to fill the tenders of the locomotives, was redundant when the top picture was taken in January 1964. It stood on the site later occupied by the canning factory, Springfield Road. In the distance you can see the shop on the corner of Victoria Street. With the press of a button, the tower which had been a landmark since 1937 came crashing down. Originally built as American Can in 1969, the can-making factory closed as Impress in 2006 and was demolished for housing development the following year. The bottom picture shows progress in 2012.

BMARCO's Springfield Road Factory, 1980, Taken from Baird's Maltings

The munitions-maker became a major employer when it came to Grantham in 1938. During the Second World War, it was the target of German bombers on several occasions. At one time it employed a workforce of 7,000 including Polish refugees.

It closed in 1993 and was bought by a consortium of local businessmen with a view to developing the land as an industrial and retail park. The latter plan failed after Deputy Prime Minister John Prescott declared this would be 'out-of-town' shopping and refused the development, so the remaining land was sold for housing. The picture taken in 2010 shows care home Brick Kiln Place being built on the site with housing developments in the background. Both pictures were taken from Baird's Maltings.

Corner of Manthorpe Road/Brook Street/Castlegate, Looking East, 1904
The houses to the left have changed little, other than the windows, while shops have been converted to houses. The shop on the right, where former Bishop of London John Wand grew up, was demolished to make way for a filling station and convenience store.

Waggon & Horses

The Waggon & Horses was a Victorian pub surviving until the twenty-first century, but only just. The top picture was taken in 2004, but six years later it had been demolished, with terraced houses built on the site of the pub and its generous car park and stables.

Harrowby Methodist Church

Harrowby Methodist Church, which began life as a wooden shed, became so popular at the turn of the millennium it was one of the fastest growing churches in the country. In 1963, the timber building which had served them since the estate was built in the 1940s, was replaced by a brick building (bottom right) housing 130 worshippers. The £10,000 improvement was built around the previous one. However, by the 1990s it was evident that the congregation had even outgrown this one. Costing £780,000, the latest church opened in March 2004.

Pensions Corner

The junction of New Beacon Road and Harrowby Road is known as Pensions Corner, after the hospital that stood there. It was set up by the Ministry of Pensions in 1921. Predating New Beacon Road, it was set in 15 acres, utilising much of the officers' mess of the former Harrowby Army Camp. It could house up to 300 patients, each ward having 20 beds. Patients had their own cricket and bowls teams. It closed in 1930 and patients were transferred to Orpington. In 1953, eight shops were built by Foster & Son with flats above them which remain to this day.

Grantham Civic Trust

Members of Grantham Civic Trust taskforce and local youngsters with some of the rubbish taken out of the Grantham Canal near Earlesfield Lane bridge in 1969. Unfortunately, in 2012, a swan finds little has changed.

Bjorlow Ltd, Earlesfield Lane

Five hundred jobs were created at Bjorlow (Great Britain) Ltd tannery when it opened on Earlesfield Lane in 1934. The Danish company had taken over the premises of Alexander Shaw, which had gone bust three years earlier after nearly seventy years. Leatherworking had been a continuous trade in Grantham from medieval times until the demise of Bjorlow's in 1973. The old buildings were demolished and Hollis Road industrial estate rose in its place.

Beeden Park

Beeden Park was billed as a 'Garden City' when work began in 1939. The houses, which fronted Dysart Road between Grantham and Barrowby, were known as the 'Flat-Tops' as they had flat concrete roofs. The first completed were for workers associated with the war effort. In 1988, they were 'Flat-Tops' no more, following a £309,000 programme of improvements which included installing pitched roofs.

Harrow Street

Harrow Street backyards in 1905 were a great adventure for the children playing there. Most of the old houses have disappeared and been replaced by modern residences.

Aveling Barford

Aveling Barford was a giant engineering force, although the company was liquidated in 1988 and successor Wordsworth Holdings followed in 2010. It arrived in Grantham in 1933. Post-war, the company developed a new breed of road rollers, powered by diesel engines, and spearheaded a worldwide export drive, chartering whole trains to take its goods to the docks. A large earth grader was added to the list of products and the size of dumpers continued to grow eventually to 40-ton giants. The company became the town's biggest employer with a workforce of more than 3,000.

By 1983, when the firm was bought by Singapore rubber tycoon Dr Lee Kin Tat, it had only 800 employees and turnover had dropped to £30 million, about half of what it had been a decade earlier.

Bombing II

Thirty-two people were killed and forty-one injured – nearly half of them seriously – in an air raid in October 1942. The sirens sounded at 9.30 p.m. when two German bombers were spotted. When the planes dropped flares, it was said to be like daytime. The first two high-explosive bombs were believed to be targeting Bomber Command HQ at St Vincent's but one fell in the road in Bridge Street. The second was the more serious. An air raid shelter in Bridge Street took a direct hit and was demolished together with a score of homes, killing twenty people. An eye witness said: 'Dust, glass and bricks were scattered randomly with bleeding, mutilated bodies, limbs no longer attached and unrecognisable pieces of human bodies lying everywhere. The air was rent with the screams of the injured victims and shouts of rescuers.' Builders were taken off the Beeden Park building site to dig extra graves for the casualties.

St John's Church

Mayor of Grantham Councillor Montague Ogden and entourage arrive at St John's Church for the 1967 St George's Day service. Many of the buildings in the background, mainly Commercial Road and Launder Terrace, have since disappeared. One of them is part of Lee & Grinling's Commercial Road maltings. On the side of the building it states Church Terrace, although most people know this short-cut from London Road to the railway station as Nursery Path.

Alford Street

Alford Street was judged the best decorated street in town at the time of the Coronation in 1953, with abundant bunting and even flower tubs. However, their enthusiasm seemed to have waned by the time the Diamond Jubilee came along in 2012. Only a solitary Union Flag in neighbouring Redcross Street hints that something is going on.